# From Solo Leadership to Team Empowerment

## *10 Transformative Shifts for Modern Leaders*

Kenneth M. Rollins

Table of Contents

# Introduction: The Evolution from Leadership to Team Empowerment

In today's ever-changing world of organizational dynamics, the classic concept of leadership as a solo, top-down job is losing relevance. The world has become too complicated for anyone to have all the answers or bear the decision-making load. Instead, today's most successful leaders recognize the value of building strong, collaborative teams. They understand that leadership is no longer about standing outside the group, but about being deeply ingrained in it, directing from within rather than above.

The rise of teamwork

Teamwork is a paradigm change in how we think about leadership and work. At its foundation, teamship is about adopting a collaborative approach in which each team member plays an important part in achieving success. This paradigm shifts from the old-fashioned notion of a single, heroic leader to one in which leadership is diffused, contributions are valued equally, and collective knowledge drives decision-making.

This transition is more than simply a response to changes in workplace culture; it is a requirement in an age marked by fast technology breakthroughs, varied workforce dynamics, and an increasing demand for agility and creativity. Teams that flourish under empowered leadership are more prepared to adapt to obstacles, stimulate innovation, and generate long-term success.

## Why Shift is Critical

Leaders who insist on antiquated, individualistic techniques risk alienating their workforce, impeding innovation, and restricting organizational potential. Leadership is no longer about demanding obedience; rather, it is about encouraging cooperation. Today's leader must be a catalyst—someone who allows others to shine, fosters trust and creates an atmosphere in which every person feels appreciated and inspired to achieve their full potential.

## 10 Transformative Changes for Leaders

This book is a resource for leaders who want to embrace the future by shifting from solo leadership to team empowerment. Each chapter focuses on one of the 10 transformational transformations required to make this transition. These transformations are about more than simply changing methods; they are about redefining the leadership attitude itself. They challenge leaders to:

Move from having power to developing influence.

Shift your focus from task management to creativity.

Move from focusing on individual accomplishments to recognizing group achievements.

Learn to cooperate, coach, and co-create instead of dictating.

What You'll Discover

This book offers practical ideas, real-world examples, and tangible tactics for becoming a team-focused leader. You'll learn to:

Create a culture of trust and cooperation.

Encourage your staff to take responsibility and innovate.

Focus on long-term, collaborative development rather than short-term gains.

The Power of Team Empowerment

This path is about more than simply becoming a better leader; it is about unleashing your team's full potential. When leadership is shared, teams become more motivated, resilient, and capable of conquering obstacles collectively. As a result, leaders feel less burnout and more fulfilled when they see their people accomplish great things.

It is time to redefine leadership as a collaborative journey rather than a single quest. This book will teach you how to lead with purpose, empower your team, and create a culture of success for everyone involved. Welcome to the realm of team empowerment. Let us begin.

# From Command to Collaboration: A New Era of Leadership

For millennia, leadership has been associated with authority. Command-and-control structures were the foundation of organizations, with choices taken at the top and commands cascading down like edicts from the monarch. In this approach, the leader had absolute control, and the team was expected to execute directions precisely. While this method may have succeeded in the industrial period, when efficiency and obedience were valued above all else, it is becoming more useless in today's dynamic, fast-paced, and innovation-oriented society.

Modern teams thrive on cooperation rather than command. The days of inflexible hierarchies are over, giving way to nimble, adaptable organizations that prioritize shared decision-making and mutual respect. This transition from command to collaboration is more than a trend; it is a must for organizations aiming to stay competitive, inventive, and resilient in an age marked by complexity and change.

Downfall of the Command Model

The command paradigm is based on the notion that the person at the top knows best. While this may have been true in an era when information was limited and leadership was essentially about carrying out repetitious chores, it fails in a world where knowledge is dispersed, issues are complicated, and solutions need multiple viewpoints.

Command-based architectures often result in:

1. Bottlenecked Decision-Making: When all decisions are routed via a single leader, progress slows and opportunities are lost.

2. Disengaged Teams: Employees who believe their views are ignored or appreciated are less likely to share their greatest ideas.

3. Resistance to Change: A lack of teamwork creates a climate in which teams are more prone to fight commands than to embrace them.

The Case for Collaboration

Collaboration alters how teams work. Instead of depending on a single person for guidance, collaborative settings use the team's combined intellect, creativity, and enthusiasm. This method moves the emphasis from control to empowerment, allowing teams to flourish in ways traditional command hierarchies cannot.

1. Shared Decision-Making Leads to Better Results.

When team members participate in decision-making, they bring unique views, talents, and experiences to the table. This variety not only enhances the decision-making process but also lowers the likelihood of blind spots and prejudice. Collaborative decision-making encourages buy-in, ensuring that the whole team is committed to the conclusion.

2. Mutual respect promotes engagement.

Collaboration flourishes in circumstances where mutual respect is the foundation. Leaders who listen to and appreciate their team members' opinions foster a culture of trust. Employees in such circumstances feel empowered to express their ideas, question assumptions, and make important contributions. This attitude of respect and inclusion promotes engagement, resulting in increased productivity and happiness.

3. Agility in the Face of Change

Teams that work together are better able to adapt to changes. When everyone has a voice and knows the reasoning behind choices, they are more likely to welcome change and collaborate to make it successful. Collaboration builds resilience, allowing teams to handle unpredictability with confidence.

Developing a Collaborative Culture

The transition from command to cooperation demands deliberate effort. It necessitates a redesign of leadership roles, team interactions, and organizational structures. Here's how leaders can create a collaborative environment:

1. Define leadership as facilitation.

The collaborative leader serves as a facilitator, not a commander. Their responsibility is to set the stage for success by guiding conversations and ensuring that every team member's voice is heard. They define the vision while allowing the team to take its route.

2. Encourage open communication.

Collaboration thrives in circumstances where communication is clear and open. Leaders must provide areas for open discussion, where ideas may be offered without fear of being judged. Regular team meetings, brainstorming sessions, and one-on-one check-ins are all effective techniques for encouraging open communication.

3. Accept diverse perspectives.

Collaboration relies on diversity to function. Leaders should aggressively seek and respect varied opinions, regardless of cultural origin, area of expertise, or personal experiences. Teams that embrace diversity may provide innovative answers to complicated situations.

4. Provide Teams with Autonomy

Micromanagement is the opponent of cooperation. To promote a collaborative culture, leaders must empower their staff to make choices and accept responsibility for their work. This requires a willingness to delegate authority and allow team members to lead in their areas of competence.

5. Acknowledge and celebrate contributions.

Recognizing team members' efforts and successes helps to promote a collaborative atmosphere. When people believe their contributions are recognized, they are more likely to remain engaged and involved in the team's success.

Real-Life Examples of Collaboration in Action

The transition from command to collaboration is more than just theoretical; it is already changing organizations across sectors.

Google's focus on psychological safety and collaborative problem-solving has been a key component of its success. Google has continually fostered creativity by creating an atmosphere in which team members feel comfortable taking chances and sharing ideas.

Pixar's creative process is built on teamwork. Directors, animators, and writers collaborate in iterative cycles, analyzing and improving each other's work to create some of history's most popular films.

Agile Software Development: The agile technique, which emphasizes collaboration, flexibility, and continual feedback, has transformed the way software is built. Teams operate in sprints, collaborating to solve issues and produce value progressively.

## Challenges of Collaboration

While cooperation has many advantages, it is not without obstacles. Leaders could encounter:

Conflicts may arise as a result of differing points of view. Effective leaders must actively arbitrate disagreements to maximize their potential for creativity.

Decision-Making Delays: If collaboration is not properly handled, it may slow down decision-making. Leaders need to achieve a balance between inclusion and efficiency.

Ego Clashes: Leaders must carefully negotiate egos, ensuring that no one voice takes precedence and that all contributions are treated equally.

The Future of Leadership Is Collaborative

The transition from command to collaboration is more than just a change in management style; it involves a fundamental reassessment of what it means to lead. In a world that requires adaptation, innovation, and resilience, cooperation is essential for teams to reach their full potential.

By accepting this transformation, leaders can foster settings in which people are empowered, teams are engaged, and organizations prosper. Collaboration is more than simply a tactic; it is the cornerstone of contemporary leadership. As leaders, the issue is no more whether we should cooperate, but rather how successfully we can lead with collaboration at the forefront of our efforts.

# From Visionary to Vision-Builder: The Art of Co-Creating a Shared Future

For many years, the paradigm of the leader as a lone visionary has been revered in leadership literature. We admire people like Steve Jobs, Elon Musk, and other fearless visionaries who seemed to glimpse the future before anybody else and single-handedly forged a road to success. However, the reality is significantly more convoluted. While having a vision is necessary for leadership, the ability to engage people in that vision—to co-create a common purpose—distinguishes the truly transformational leader.

Transitioning from a solo visionary to a vision-builder entails shifting away from establishing and imposing a vision and towards including your team in the process. The goal is to enhance the leader's insight by using the group's collective expertise, creativity, and dedication. This method guarantees that team members have a strong feeling of responsibility and are aligned with organizational objectives.

Why the Shift Matters

1. Ownership promotes commitment.

People who participate in the vision-creation process are more likely to experience a feeling of ownership. A vision sent down from above might seem remote, abstract, or even irrelevant to team members' everyday lives. In contrast, a collaborative vision takes on a personal dimension. Team members identify with the vision, which fuels the intrinsic desire to contribute to its realization.

2.     Alignment ensures cohesion.

Co-creating a vision ensures that everyone knows and supports the organization's aims. It bridges the gap between leadership goals and team execution, reducing misunderstandings and misalignment.

3. Collective wisdom improves vision.

No leader, no matter how smart, can equal the combined intellect of a motivated, diverse team. When leaders include their teams in vision-building, they get access to a wealth of ideas, views, and experiences that may enhance and strengthen the vision.

4. Adapting to a Complex World.

Organizations confront more complex and rapidly changing issues. A vision developed by a single individual in solitude risks being outrun by reality. Collaborative vision-building enables organizations to stay flexible and adaptable by using the team's collective capacity to foresee and react to change.

How to Go from Visionary to Vision Builder

Making the transition to a vision-builder involves deliberate work, humility, and a willingness to share responsibility and credit. Here's how leaders can establish a compelling vision with their teams:

1. Start with core values.

Every vision must be based on the organization's basic beliefs. As a leader, you set the tone by clearly communicating these beliefs. However, integrating your team in defining how these principles apply to everyday activities and long-term objectives lays a solid basis for co-creation.

For example, a technology company may value innovation, but how does this manifest itself in practice? Team workshops allow you to collaboratively define what "innovation" means in your unique environment, ensuring everyone has a common understanding.

2. Paint the Big Picture, but Leave Room for Input.

As a leader, you provide the first framework—a broad picture of where the organization should go. This is the beginning point of the conversation, not the last word.

Express your vision via a tale or narrative.

Invite your team to fill in the gaps, question assumptions, and improve the details.

By allowing for input, you promote creativity and a feeling of shared ownership.

3. Facilitate open dialogue.

Open and honest discussion is essential for effective vision-building. Leaders must establish safe environments in which team members feel comfortable expressing ideas and raising concerns.

Use brainstorming sessions, seminars, or retreats to get your staff involved in the visioning process.

Ask thought-provoking questions, such as:

What motivates you in our present direction?

What difficulties do you perceive that we should address?

How can we make our vision more inclusive and actionable?

4. Utilize Diverse Perspectives.

A varied staff gives a variety of viewpoints that may contribute to the vision.

Encourage contributions from all levels of the organization, so that every voice is heard.

Leaders should aggressively solicit feedback from departments, jobs, and backgrounds that may be under-represented.

Diversity in vision-building guarantees that the resultant vision is shared within the organization and meets a broader range of needs and possibilities.

5. Collaborate on Measurable Goals

A vision without practical objectives is only a dream. Once the broad vision has been defined, collaborate with your team to boil it down into specific, quantifiable targets. This method not only makes the idea more real but also strengthens group ownership.

Determine significant milestones and KPIs as a group.

To establish responsibility, assign roles and tasks cooperatively.

6. Communicate The Vision Relentlessly

To thrive, a common vision must be reinforced on a regular basis. Leaders must serve as primary storytellers, constantly reminding the team of the goal and how their job fits into it.

Reinforce the vision via all channels of communication, including meetings, emails, one-on-ones, and public forums.

Celebrate progress towards the goal to sustain momentum and morale.

7. Empower your team to lead.

Being a vision builder entails acknowledging that leadership is not limited to a single individual. Encourage team members to take ownership of the vision in their areas of expertise.

Delegate decision-making power where appropriate.

Encourage initiative and creativity that are consistent with the goal.

8. Work together to adapt and refine.

A vision does not remain static; it must adapt as circumstances change. To ensure that the vision stays current and compelling, have your team evaluate and refine it on a regular basis.

Hold quarterly or yearly vision check-ins to get input and make changes.

Recognize and absorb lessons from achievements and disappointments.

Real-World Examples of Vision Building

Satya Nadella at Microsoft: When Nadella became CEO, he unveiled a new vision of "empowering every person and organization on the planet to achieve more." Instead of prescribing this vision, he worked with teams throughout the organization to improve and execute it, resulting in a significant cultural and strategic revolution.

Patagonia's concept is profoundly rooted in environmental sustainability. Leadership actively engages people in defining and carrying out this vision via collaborative initiatives, ensuring congruence with both organizational aims and personal interests.

Challenges of Co-Creation

While vision-building has several benefits, it is not without challenges:

Time-consuming:
Collaborative approaches may take longer than top-down choices. Leaders must strike a balance between the need for feedback and the urgency of action.

Conflict Resolution: Disagreements may arise when people have different points of view. Leaders must resolve these disagreements constructively in order to retain unity.

Balancing Inclusivity and Clarity: While it is critical to incorporate everyone, leaders must keep the goal clear and focused.

The payoff: A vision that inspires and endures.

When leaders transform from lonely visionaries to vision-builders, they generate something much more powerful than a vision statement: a movement. A common vision not only unifies and stimulates teams, but also serves as a guidepost for overcoming obstacles and seizing opportunities.

Co-creating a vision turns leadership into a collaborative effort in which all team members feel seen, heard, and respected. It's a move that promotes trust, increases engagement, and creates the groundwork for long-term success.

As a leader, your greatest legacy is the vision you create with your team—a vision that lasts because it belongs to everyone.

# From Authority to Influence: The Power of Authentic Leadership

In older leadership styles, authority was paramount. Leaders are influenced because of their titles, jobs, or positions, and their teams are expected to obey commands without question. The organizational hierarchy positioned leaders at the top, imposing their will via directives and control. But things have changed. The era of authority-driven leadership is making way for a more nuanced, dynamic approach: leadership by influence.

Influence is not derived from a title or position; rather, it comes from trust, sincerity, and the capacity to inspire others. The transition from authority to influence is more than a trend; it's a must in an era when cooperation, innovation, and engagement drive success. In a world where liberty and authenticity are valued, leaders must learn to inspire rather than impose, and advise rather than control.

This transformation necessitates leaders trading the ease of control for the difficulty of connection. It requires humility, emotional intelligence, and a willingness to engage in developing connections. In this chapter, we look at why this change is important, how to implement it, and what it looks like in reality.

Why Moving from Authority to Influence is Important

1. Authority is finite; influence is enduring.

Authority is linked to position and power dynamics. It might be transient and confined to certain situations. Influence, on the other hand, goes beyond titles. It is founded on respect, trust, and connections that endure even when positions change.

A management who is primarily focused on their title may struggle to lead after leaving the organization, but a leader who has established influence will continue to inspire followers wherever they go.

2. Modern teams stress empowerment over obedience.

Today's workforce, particularly millennials and Generation Z, wants to be treated as equals rather than subordinates.

They choose leaders who listen, empower, and facilitate their development rather than merely issuing commands.

Employees are more engaged when they believe their efforts are valued and their opinions are heard.

Command-and-control leadership may alienate brilliant people who value individuality and innovation.

3.      Influence promotes collaboration and innovation.

Authority-driven leadership may hinder cooperation by instilling fear and suppressing opposition. Influential leaders create an atmosphere in which team members feel comfortable sharing ideas, challenging assumptions, and innovating without fear of repercussions.

Influence promotes cooperation, which leads to more creative ideas and better solutions.

Trust-based leadership fosters an open atmosphere in which errors are recognized as learning opportunities rather than failures that must be penalized.

4. Influence Enhances Resilience

In times of crisis, power alone is seldom adequate. Teams need leaders who can inspire confidence and mobilize people behind a common goal. Influence enables leaders to encourage and unify their staff in the face of uncertainty.

The foundation of influence is trust and authenticity.

At the core of influence is trust. Without it, no amount of charm or persuasion can make a lasting impression. Building trust requires authenticity—being honest, truthful, and consistent in your behavior.

1. Be genuine.

Authentic leaders remain loyal to themselves and their convictions. They don't put up a front or claim to be flawless. Instead, they exhibit vulnerability, accept errors, and showcase compassion.

For example, a leader who freely recognizes obstacles and solicits feedback is more respected than one who claims to have all of the solutions.

Authenticity develops stronger ties because team members see their leader as approachable and trustworthy.

2. Show empathy.

Empathy is the capacity to comprehend and share the emotions of others. It is a cornerstone of influence because it communicates that you value your team members as persons rather than simply employees.

Listen actively to grasp their needs, problems, and goals.

Use empathy to personalize your leadership style, making sure that every team member feels appreciated and supported.

3. Act with integrity.

Influence thrives on the regularity of words and acts. Leaders who behave with integrity—keeping commitments, being fair, and

adhering to their values—
develop trust over time.

Integrity establishes a solid moral basis, inspiring loyalty and respect.

Leaders who prioritize integrity establish an environment of honesty and accountability inside their organizations.

How to Move From Authority to Influence.

1. Change from "commanding" to "guiding"

Authority-driven leaders issue commands, whereas influence-driven leaders offer counsel. Instead of instructing their teams what to do, powerful leaders ask questions, give information, and empower them to make their judgments.

Coach team members on how to solve difficulties and build their talents.

Provide clear objectives while allowing people to choose how to attain them.

2. Establish Relationships Before Results

Relationships serve as the foundation for influence. Take the time to understand your team members on a personal level, including their abilities, interests, and motivations.

Create a feeling of belonging by celebrating accomplishments and acknowledging efforts.

Create chances for team bonding, such as frequent check-ins, team-building exercises, or casual discussions.

3. Lead by example.

Setting the norm establishes credibility, which is required for influence. Be the leader that you want your team to imitate.

Showcase a strong work ethic, an optimistic outlook, and a dedication to excellence.

Show humility by asking comments and being willing to grow.

4. Empower others.

Authority concentrates power at the top, while influence spreads it throughout the team. Delegating responsibility, trusting team members, and encouraging them to take ownership of their work are all ways to empower others.

Assign hard assignments and encourage skill improvement to provide opportunities for advancement.

Encourage team members to take the initiative and recognize their efforts.

5. Communicate with clarity and purpose.

Influential leaders are excellent communicators. They communicate their goal effectively, elicit excitement, and give constant feedback.

Use storytelling to build emotional connections with your team.

Align your communication with the team's beliefs and objectives to create a shared feeling of purpose.

Challenges of Influence-Driven Leadership

The transition from power to influence is not without problems. It takes patience, emotional intelligence, and a willingness to let go of control. Leaders must

Overcome opposition from team members who are used to established hierarchies.

Negotiate problems and disagreements with diplomacy and tact.

Balance the urge for influence with the need to make difficult choices when necessary.

Real-World Examples of Leadership Via Influence

1. Jacinda Ardern.

Jacinda Ardern, New Zealand's Prime Minister, led with empathy, honesty, and sincerity. Her capacity to interact with individuals on a personal basis helped her become a worldwide recognized leader, particularly during times of crisis, such as the COVID-19 epidemic.

2. Nelson Mandela.

Mandela's leadership was based on persuasion rather than authority. Despite years in jail, he emerged as a uniting figure, inspiring millions with his goal of forgiveness and equality.

3) Satya Nadella

Nadella transformed Microsoft's culture from competitive and compartmentalized to collaborative and growth-oriented. His impact was founded on empathy, humility, and a commitment to empowering workers.

The Payoff: Influence creates impact.

When leaders go from power to influence, they unlock their teams' full potential. Influence-driven leadership promotes trust, cooperation, and creativity, resulting in a culture in which people feel appreciated, empowered, and inspired.

Authority may force obedience but influence fosters commitment. It's a transformation that not only alters the way leaders lead, but also redefines what leadership means in a society that values honesty, connection, and purpose.

# From Manager to Mentor: Nurturing Growth Beyond the Task List

In the business sector, the function of a manager has long been linked with task supervision, meeting deadlines, and keeping the team on track with organizational objectives. It's all about structure, methods, and demonstrable results. However, as workplaces develop, so do the expectations of leadership. Teams are increasingly looking for a mentor, not just a manager, who will invest in their personal and professional development, leading them to reach their full potential and accomplish their goals.

The journey from manager to mentor is more than just a change in responsibility; it is a fundamental adjustment in thinking and approach. It is necessary to go beyond transactional relationships focused on tasks and instead establish deep, meaningful ties that inspire trust, create development, and enable people to flourish.

Why the Transition from Manager to Mentor Matters

1. The workforce is changing.

Employees today, particularly millennials and Generation Z, place a high importance on development, purpose, and connection. They are less driven by hierarchical authority and more inspired by leaders who invest in their growth.

According to surveys, professional development possibilities are one of the most important things workers evaluate when deciding whether or not to remain in a position.

Employees want their leaders to be coaches who guide them toward their objectives rather than taskmasters who just direct their work.

2. Mentorship promotes engagement and retention.

Mentorship extends beyond project accomplishment; it fosters loyalty and involvement. Employees who feel encouraged in their development are more likely to remain with their organization.

According to Gallup data, mentored workers are more engaged, productive, and likely to remain with their employer for longer periods.

Mentorship promotes a feeling of belonging and purpose, which reduces turnover and strengthens organizational cultures.

3. Developing individuals leads to organizational success.

When managers prioritize mentoring their team members, they generate a ripple effect that benefits the whole organization. Skilled, motivated personnel stimulate innovation, increase production, and contribute to a good work environment.

Mentorship enables people to think critically, take responsibility, and give ideas, thus promoting continual growth.

Organizations that prioritize mentorship perceive improved performance, teamwork, and flexibility.

Key Differences Between Managing and Mentoring

1. Task-Centric vs People-Centric.

Managers concentrate on completing tasks, meeting deadlines, and attaining immediate goals.

Mentor: Prioritises individual growth and development, understanding that their success adds to the team's and organization's long-term objectives.

2. Directing versus Guiding

Manager: Issues directions and oversees execution.

Mentor: Encourages autonomy, assists people in developing their solutions, and acts as a sounding board for ideas and issues.

3. Evaluating vs Empowering.

Manager: Evaluates performance using measurements and outcomes.

Mentor: Emphasizes potential, providing comments and opportunities to learn, develop, and overcome constraints.

How to Transition from Manager to Mentor.

1. Build trust as the foundation.

Trust is the foundation of all mentoring relationships. Without it, team members would not feel comfortable asking for advice or expressing their goals and difficulties.

Be authentic: Demonstrate to your staff that you care about their success, not simply their productivity.

Be Consistent: Keep your promises and foster an atmosphere in which team members feel secure to be themselves.

Be Approachable: Encourage open conversation and be willing to listen and provide help.

2. Concentrate on individual goals.

Mentorship starts with a grasp of each team member's individual goals, abilities, and problems.

Engage in one-on-one interactions to discover their personal and professional aspirations.

Align their ambitions with organizational aims, resulting in a win-win situation.

Provide chances based on their interests, such as training programs, stretch assignments, or networking contacts.

3. Switch from Feedback to Feedforward

Managers often evaluate previous performance, while mentors emphasize future potential.

Provide constructive criticism that emphasizes chances for progress.

Use feedforward approaches, which concentrate on what team members can do to attain their objectives rather than lingering on previous failures.

Encourage introspection, allowing team members to learn from their experiences and apply those lessons in the future.

4. Promote autonomy and decision-making.

A manager may feel forced to monitor every choice, but a mentor allows their team to take responsibility and learn from the experience.

Delegate significant duties, allowing team members to lead and make choices.

Help people overcome obstacles by offering suggestions rather than answers.

Celebrate their triumphs to boost their confidence and capabilities.

5. Invest in continuous learning.

Mentors are lifelong learners who encourage their teams to adopt the same approach.

Share your own experiences and lessons learned to give relevant insights.

Encourage team members to explore new skills, views, and possibilities.

Give them access to materials like books, courses, and professional networks that will help them grow.

Challenges of Becoming a Mentor

1.    Balancing    short-term results with long-term growth.

Managers are often under pressure to achieve fast results. Investing in mentoring may seem like a luxury when deadlines are approaching, but it is a smart investment in long-term success.

2. Let Go of Control

Shifting from a directive to a supporting position necessitates giving up control. This might be challenging for managers who are used to controlling every detail, but it is critical for empowering team members.

3. Navigating Resistance

Some team members may be unwilling to accept mentoring, seeing it as intrusive or unneeded. It is critical to establish trust and show the usefulness of the mentoring relationship over time.

Real-World Examples of Mentoring in Action

1. Howard Schultz, Starbucks

Schultz, the CEO of Starbucks, was recognized for his mentorship-focused leadership style. He invested in his workers' development and well-being, providing possibilities for professional progression and instilling a sense of purpose inside the organization.

2) Oprah Winfrey

Oprah's success as a media mogul stems from her mentoring of numerous people, both on and off television. She encourages her staff by developing their skills, encouraging them to follow their hobbies, and setting a good example.

3. Indra Nooyi (PepsiCo).

Nooyi's term as CEO of PepsiCo was distinguished by a dedication to nurturing future leaders. She emphasized mentoring and empowerment, fostering an environment in which people felt appreciated and encouraged in their development.

The Benefits of Being a Mentor

The transition from manager to mentor alters both the leader and the team. It provides the leader with the gratification of having a long-term effect on the lives of others. For the team, it fosters a supportive atmosphere in which people feel encouraged to realize their full potential.

Mentors leave a leadership legacy by ensuring the success of the people they have coached.

Mentorship promotes a culture of learning, creativity, and cooperation, resulting in long-term organizational success.

The Manager-Mentor Duality.

While the responsibilities of manager and mentor may seem to be mutually incompatible, they are not. A genuinely successful leader smoothly blends both, managing work and coaching people. Leaders who transition from a transactional to a transformational approach may encourage their people to not only meet but also surpass expectations. The change from boss to mentor is not easy, but it is worthwhile. It's a move that strengthens connections, improves performance, and fosters a workplace culture in which employees are encouraged to develop, prosper, and lead.

# From Independence to Interdependence:

# Building a Collaborative Force

Independence has long been seen as a symbol of strength and self-reliance, particularly in individualistic countries. It reflects the capacity to work independently, accept responsibility, and achieve success via own effort. However, in today's linked world, independence is no longer adequate for success in complicated and dynamic contexts.

Interdependence—the capacity to rely on and contribute to others—is the next step towards successful cooperation. It is the realization that collective accomplishment outweighs individual effort, and that genuine power resides in leveraging a group's unique talents. This transition from independence to dependency is about more than simply working together; it's about developing connections, nurturing trust, and creating a culture of cooperation that fosters creativity and shared success.

The Value of Interdependence in Modern Teams

1. The nature of work has changed.

Organizations nowadays confront complicated difficulties that need a wide range of viewpoints and experience. No one person, regardless of ability or experience, can master all aspects of contemporary problem-solving.

Interdependent teams bring together diverse abilities, resulting in a synergy that leads to more robust solutions.

Collaborative spaces promote creative thinking by enabling people to build on one another's ideas.

2. Independence creates silos.

When people or departments operate independently, silos arise, resulting in inefficiencies and confusion.

Interdependence removes these boundaries, promoting cross-functional cooperation.

Silos impede the flow of information and resources, while interdependence encourages openness and knowledge exchange.

Teams that value interdependence are more flexible, adaptive, and focused on organizational objectives.

3. Interdependence strengthens relationships.

Strong teams are founded on trust and mutual respect. Interdependence fosters these attributes, resulting in a feeling of belonging and oneness.

Collaboration increases understanding and respect for each team member's efforts.

Interdependence creates a culture of support in which people feel valued and empowered.

The transition from independence to interdependence.

1. Recognising the limitations of independence.

The first step towards dependency is to recognize that independence, although desirable, has its limits.

Independent achievers often face unreasonable expectations, which may lead to burnout.

When team members operate in silos, they may lose out on chances to use one another's skills.

2. Seeing collaboration as a strength.

Interdependence is not a weakness, but rather a strategic asset. Leaders need to transform the narrative from "doing it alone" to "achieving together."

Collaboration multiplies individual efforts, resulting in outputs that are beyond what any one person could accomplish.

Teams that value interdependence are more resilient because they can draw on shared resources and assistance.

3. Establishing a Culture of Trust and Mutual Respect

Trust is the basis for interdependence. Without it, people would be hesitant to depend on others or share their thoughts.

Foster Psychological Safety: Create an atmosphere in which team members feel comfortable expressing themselves without fear of judgment or punishment.

Encourage Vulnerability: Leaders may demonstrate vulnerability by acknowledging their limits and soliciting feedback from their teams.

The pillars of interdependence
1. Complementary strengths
Interdependence flourishes when team members recognize and respect each other's abilities.

Identify Skills: Map out the team's different skills and ensure that duties are linked with individual abilities.

Celebrate Differences: Encourage team members to see differences as advantages rather than disadvantages.

## 2. Shared Goals

A shared vision binds people, directing their efforts towards a single goal.

Define objectives. Setting objectives along with the team may help to create ownership and commitment.

Measure Collective Success: Prioritize results that represent the team's overall success above individual accomplishments.

## 3. Open communication

Transparent and honest communication is vital for establishing trust and teamwork.

Encourage Dialogue: Give team members frequent opportunities to exchange ideas, offer feedback, and address issues.

Resolve Conflicts Constructively: Address conflicts quickly and utilize them to enhance relationships.

## 4. Accountability and Support

Interdependence necessitates striking a balance between keeping each other responsible and offering assistance when required.

Mutual accountability: Encourage team members to accept responsibility for their contributions and obligations.

Provide Assistance: Foster a culture in which asking for assistance is seen as a sign of strength, not weakness.

Challenges of Fostering Interdependence.

1. Fear of losing control.

Individuals who are used to independence may be resistant to interdependence for fear of losing their autonomy.

Leaders may counter this by emphasizing that interconnectedness strengthens, not undermines, individual contributions.

2. Misaligned expectations.

Interdependence necessitates clarity on roles, duties, and expectations. Without this, misunderstanding and dissatisfaction may occur.

Regularly review and align on team objectives, ensuring that everyone knows their role in accomplishing them.

3. Overcoming Ego and Competition.

Individuals in highly competitive workplaces may find it difficult to choose team achievement above personal recognition.

Leaders should encourage teamwork and provide possibilities for mutual achievement.

The Benefits of Interdependence

1. Enhanced Performance

Teams that accept interdependence do better than those that rely simply on individual effort.

Interdependence promotes speedier problem resolution, higher-quality outputs, and more creativity.

Collaborative teams are stronger at adapting to change and overcoming obstacles.

2. Stronger relationships.

Interdependence provides a feeling of community and

belonging, which helps to build team connections.

Employees who feel linked to their coworkers are more engaged, driven, and pleased with their jobs.

3. A Culture of Growth.

Interdependence fosters an atmosphere in which people may learn from one another, expanding their talents and views.

Teams that prioritize cooperation promote ongoing learning and growth.

Real-world examples of interdependence

1. Pixar Animation Studios.

Pixar's success is due in large part to its collaborative culture. To make breakthrough films, the firm fosters free communication and draws on its broad team's capabilities.

Regular "braintrust" sessions provide a comfortable environment for team members to exchange comments and ideas.

2. The Apollo 11 mission.

The accomplishment of the Apollo 11 lunar landing demonstrated interdependence. Scientists, engineers, and astronauts collaborated to accomplish a common objective by using each other's knowledge.

The mission's complexity necessitated seamless coordination across disciplines and organizations.

The Power of We.

The transition from independence to interdependence reflects a significant change in how teams operate and perform. It is about transcending beyond individual success and recognizing the potential of group effort.

Interdependence does not lessen the value of independence; rather, it strengthens it by providing chances for people to contribute their abilities to something larger. It promotes trust, creativity, and shared prosperity.

In a world where cooperation is essential, the future belongs to teams that comprehend the full power of "we." Leaders who encourage interdependence may help their teams reach their greatest potential and produce amazing results.

# From Individual Achievement to Collective Wins: The Shift That Transforms Teams

In a culture that often celebrates the lone achiever—the star athlete, the computing genius, or the charismatic CEO—it's easy to forget that no important success occurs in isolation. Every success story, no matter how individualistic it seems, is supported by the collaborative work of many. True success is seldom achieved alone, whether it is via a family supporting a desire, a team carrying out a vision, or a community uniting behind a cause.

The transition from recognizing individual accomplishments to appreciating collective victories is revolutionary. It redefines success, strengthens teams, and promotes an inclusive and respectful culture. This transformation is more than a leadership ideal; it is a must for contemporary organizations where cooperation drives innovation and sustainability.

Why Do Collective Wins Matter?

1. Teams are the foundation of success.

While individual contributions are vital, the total of a team's efforts often outweighs the influence of any one member.

Synergy Enhances Outcomes: When team members combine their abilities, they produce results that no one can accomplish alone.

Complex Problems Require Collaboration: The difficulties of today's economic and social environments necessitate a variety of viewpoints and skills.

2. Collective wins boost morale.

Celebrating team accomplishments promotes a feeling of belonging and shared purpose, so increasing morale and motivation.

When people see their efforts recognized as part of a greater goal, they feel appreciated and energized.

An emphasis on collaborative successes fosters an atmosphere in which everyone feels proud of their accomplishments.

3. Individual recognition might encourage competition.

Overemphasis on individual accomplishments might unwittingly foster rivalries and undermine collaboration.

Healthy Rivalry vs. Toxic Rivalry: While some rivalry

may be beneficial, unbridled individuality can damage trust and teamwork.

Focus on "We" above "Me": Collective victories guarantee that team members prioritize collective achievement above individual glory.

The Evolution of Individual to Team-Centric Celebrations

1. Understanding the Role of the Team in Every Success

Even individual accomplishments are never genuinely unique. For example:

A salesperson's record-breaking quarter is contingent on the marketing team's campaigns, the product team's inventions, and the support team's devotion.

A researcher's breakthrough is often the product of years of collaborative work with colleagues and mentors.

2. Redefining Leadership's Role.

Leaders play an important part in this change by recognizing and applauding the collaborative work that drives every accomplishment.

From attention to Shared Light: Great leaders ensure that the attention is on the team rather than on themselves or a few people.

Creating a Ripple Effect: When leaders highlight team accomplishments, others are inspired to do the same, building a culture of collaborative appreciation.

How to Celebrate Collective Wins

1. Acknowledge everyone's contribution.

Celebrations should showcase how each team member contributed to the achievement.

Use team meetings to publicly acknowledge contributions.

Share specific anecdotes on how teamwork resulted in a victory.

2. Develop Rituals for Team Success.

Establish traditions to commemorate collective accomplishments, such as:

Group shout outs during meetings.
Team meals or trips after major accomplishments.
3. Tell a team-centric story.
Frame successes as a collaborative tale, emphasizing how cooperation enabled the outcome.
For instance, as a substitute for "Jane closed the deal," just state, "Jane, supported by the insights from marketing and the technical expertise of engineering, successfully closed the deal."
4. Distribute rewards among the team.
Whether it's incentives, prizes, or promotions, make sure the rewards match the group work.
To encourage the significance of cooperation on major projects, consider group bonuses or shared incentives.
The Impact of Celebrating Collective Wins
1. Stronger Team Dynamics
When victories are celebrated together, team members have

a greater feeling of togetherness and trust.

Encourages Collaboration: Knowing that success is a shared accomplishment inspires team members to help one another.

Reduces Silos: Celebrating shared accomplishments discourages the "us vs. them" mindset across departments.

2. Higher Employee Engagement

People are more engaged when they believe their contributions are important.

Collective celebrations demonstrate to workers that their labor is important and valuable.

Recognition promotes morale, resulting in increased production and retention rates.

3. The Culture of Inclusion

Organizations build a culture of inclusion and appreciation by focusing on team successes.

This inclusion improves the organization's capacity to

recruit and retain varied personnel.

Challenges and Solutions.

1. Balancing Individual Recognition and Team Wins

While group victories are important, individuals often want their efforts acknowledged.

Solution: Combine the two. Highlight individual efforts in light of the team's achievement.

2. Changing Established Mindsets.

Individualism has always been praised in organizations, therefore transitioning to collective acknowledgment may be met with hostility.

Solution: Educate teams on the advantages of cooperation and provide examples to show its worth.

3. Avoid Generic Celebrations

Vague or disingenuous acknowledgment might backfire, making teams feel unappreciated.

Solution: Be precise. Celebrations should be

tailored to showcase the team's unique contributions.

Real-World Examples of Celebrating Collective Success

1. NASA's Apollo program

The moon landing was one of humanity's greatest accomplishments, but NASA hailed it as a group effort. Engineers, scientists, administrators, and astronauts were all proud of their enormous feat.

2. The Pixar Brain Trust

Pixar's collaborative culture is based on recognizing group success. Their "Braintrust" workshops concentrate on developing concepts with team feedback, ensuring that each film is a collaborative success.

Moving Forward: A Call to Action.

The transition from individual performance to community success is more than a tactic; it is a mentality. It demands leaders and organizations reconsider how they define and recognize success.

Organizations that embrace this transformation may foster a culture of cooperation, inclusion, and shared purpose. Teams get stronger, morale rises, and the group's collective strength is released. Finally, celebrating communal victories reminds us of a fundamental truth: we accomplish more collectively than we ever could alone. Success is not about the individual; it is about the team. When we celebrate collaborative victories, we honor the individuals, the process, and the strength of togetherness that enabled it.

# From Directing to Enabling: Empowering Teams for Greater Success

Leadership has long been associated with control—leaders gave instructions, and teams obeyed them. This concept, although helpful in certain situations, is increasingly insufficient in today's complex and dynamic surroundings. Modern organizations demand agility, inventiveness, and resilience, which thrive when leaders shift from directing to enabling. This move reflects more than simply a change in method; it is a significant adjustment in perspective, one that recognizes individuals' and teams' unrealized potential.

This shift from a directive to an enabling leadership style is about empowering people to reach their greatest potential, not about giving up responsibilities. It is about creating an atmosphere in which team members feel comfortable taking initiative, solving challenges, and innovating. Let's go further into this key transition and see how it might transform teams, organizations, and leadership itself.

Why Does the Transition from Directing to Enabling Matter?

1. Complex problems need diverse solutions.

Modern challenges seldom have a single correct solution. The inflexible top-down approach reduces the opportunity for varied viewpoints to develop new solutions.

Empowering Problem Solving: When teams are given the ability to think critically and act independently, they can adapt creatively to changing situations.

Leveraging Expertise: Those who are closest to an issue frequently have the greatest understanding of it. Enabling leadership ensures that their insights are recognized.

2. Motivation and engagement rely on ownership.

Employees are more motivated and engaged when they feel autonomous and responsible for their job.

Beyond Compliance: Directive leadership promotes compliance while enabling leadership cultivates commitment.

Building Trust and Confidence: When teams are empowered, they feel more confident and perform better.

3. Enabling promotes innovation.

Individuals are more likely to innovate when they have the flexibility to explore, fail, and learn.

Reducing Fear of Failure: When leaders enable rather than command, they create a secure environment for innovation.

Encourages Initiative: When team members are given the authority to lead projects, they are more willing to take risks and experiment with new ideas.

Key Differences: Directing vs. Enabling

| Aspect | Directing | Enabling |
|---|---|---|
| Focus | Completing tasks as directed | Supporting team growth and innovation |
| Decision-Making | Centralized in the leader | Decentralized, shared across the team |
| Team Role | Execute orders | Take initiative and solve problems |
| Leader's Role | Provide instructions | Provide resources, guidance, and support |
| Outcomes | Short-term compliance | Long-term engagement and creativity |

How to Transition from Directing to Enabling

1. Redefine Leadership as a Supporting Role

Leaders must transform their perspective from "boss" to facilitator.

Become a Resource Provider: Rather than managing every

detail, concentrate on providing the team with the tools, information, and support it needs to succeed.

Active listening involves understanding team members' concerns and views to effectively help them.

2. Encourage a culture of autonomy.

Empowered teams flourish in an atmosphere that values and celebrates autonomy.

Delegate authority, not just tasks. Trust team members to make judgments based on their areas of expertise.

Encourage ownership: Assign people the duty of seeing initiatives through from start to finish.

3. Adopt a coaching mindset.

Consider leadership as coaching rather than demanding.

Ask questions, not just provide answers. Encourage critical thinking by directing team members toward their solutions.

Give Constructive Feedback: Help team members develop

by providing insights that improve their abilities and attitudes.

4. Establish a safe environment for experimentation.

Failure must be regarded as a learning opportunity to foster innovation.

Normalize Failure: Share experiences about your own mistakes to demonstrate resilience.

Reward Effort, Not Just Results: Encourage initiative and exploration, regardless of the outcome.

5. Invest in skill development.

Enabling leadership entails assisting team members in developing the necessary skills for success.

Provide Training Opportunities: Make available professional development resources.

Mentor Through Challenges: Serve as a mentor for team members while they confront hurdles, assisting them in growing through the process.

The Advantages of Enabling Leadership

1. Increased team resilience.

When teams are given the ability to make choices and solve issues autonomously, they become more adaptive to change.

Decentralized decision-making enables teams to react quickly to issues without relying on top-down directives.

Empowered Problem Solvers: Teams that accept responsibility for their work are better prepared to tackle hurdles.

2. Increased engagement and retention.

Employees are more likely to remain in positions where they feel respected and empowered.

Reduced Burnout: Enabling leadership delegated responsibilities, preventing the leader or any person from being overwhelmed.

Stronger Team Loyalty: Empowered team members

feel more connected to their organization.

3. Accelerated Innovation
Enabled teams are allowed to explore, which leads to discoveries that would not occur in a directed setting.

Diverse Perspectives: Collaborative approaches bring a wide range of views to the table.

Rapid prototyping: Empowered teams can rapidly test and iterate on ideas, increasing innovation.

Real-World Examples of Enabled Leadership

1. Satya Nadella at Microsoft.
When Satya Nadella became CEO of Microsoft, he changed the workplace culture from one of internal competitiveness to one of cooperation and empowerment.

Nadella emphasized trust over control, encouraging teams to take the initiative and create cross-departmental creativity.

Results: This culture revolution re-energized

Microsoft, resulting in ground-breaking advances in cloud computing and artificial intelligence.

## 2. Agile Methodology

Many organizations have embraced Agile concepts, which emphasize allowing teams to self-organize and adapt to changing conditions.

Team Ownership: Agile teams are responsible for their deliverables, with leaders serving as facilitators.

Empowered Teams: This method has been successful in a variety of areas, including software development and healthcare.

## Overcoming Challenges in Transition

### 1. Leaders Struggle to Let Go

Leaders who are used to a directive approach may struggle to let go of control.

Solution: Begin small, delegating certain choices and progressively increasing autonomy.

### 2. Teams unaccustomed to autonomy

Some teams may be reluctant to take the initiative if they are used to being guided.

Solution: Establish trust by openly stating expectations and offering assistance as they transition to more independence.

3. Balancing Freedom and Accountability.

Enabling leadership does not imply a lack of monitoring; it is about balancing freedom and accountability.

Solution: Establish explicit targets and check-ins to guarantee progress while also giving team members the freedom to accomplish outcomes.

A Call to Action: The Strength of Enabling Leadership

The transition from directing to enabling is more than simply a trend; it is a must for organizations seeking to survive in an increasingly complicated environment. Leaders unleash the full potential of their teams by enabling them to take the initiative, solve challenges, and innovate, thus creating a culture of sustained success.

As a leader, ask yourself if you are a director or a facilitator. The answer to this question might decide your team's destiny and the effect you have as a leader. Accept enabling leadership and experience the transforming power of trust, cooperation, and empowerment.

# From Fixed Roles to Dynamic Contributions: A Blueprint for Flexible and Empowered Teams

In today's quickly changing work environment, the era of strict job descriptions and defined responsibilities is giving way to a more dynamic form of cooperation. This transition reflects not just shifting market realities, but also an understanding of human potential as fluid and multidimensional. Leaders who understand and embrace this transition may help their teams achieve amazing results. But how can you go from a world of set positions to one of dynamic contributions? Let's go exploring.

Case Against Fixed Roles

Fixed jobs originated during the industrial period when efficiency was dependent on specialization and repetition. Employees were required to execute a specific job and contribute to the broader system in a consistent, assembly-line approach. This strategy worked effectively in a world where change was gradual and duties were consistent.

However, today's corporate climate is far from stagnant. Disruption is the norm, and flexibility has become an essential survival skill. Fixed positions create silos, inhibit creativity, and fail to take advantage of the many talents and interests that team members bring to the table.

The limitations of permanent roles are:

1. Stifled creativity: Employees confined to tightly defined positions may never have the opportunity to utilize their unique insights or abilities.

2. Reduced agility: Teams with strict boundaries struggle to adjust when priorities change or emergencies occur.

3. Lower engagement: When people feel underutilized, their motivation and morale diminish, resulting in disengagement.

4. Missed opportunities: Leaders may fail to recognize latent skills that might transform the organization.

Why Dynamic Contributions Matter

Employees are complicated, growing people with various talents, interests, and potential, and dynamic contributions recognize this. Organizations become more inventive, resilient, and collaborative when team members are encouraged to take on responsibilities depending on project demands and personal skills.

Key advantages of dynamic contributions:

1. Improved problem-solving: Different viewpoints may be applied to problems, leading to more innovative and effective solutions.

2. Increased resilience: When team members take on diverse tasks, organizations can better withstand unforeseen disturbances.

3. Increased ownership: When employees can contribute beyond their formal job definitions, they feel empowered, which fosters pride and responsibility.

4. Improved career development: Dynamic jobs enable individuals to pursue their interests and learn new skills, enhancing their value to the organization and improving retention.

## Developing a Culture of Flexibility

Shifting from fixed jobs to dynamic contributions requires a culture shift, not just new rules. Leaders must set the tone by fostering a workplace in which flexibility is not just welcomed but applauded.

1. Encourage a growth mindset.

A growth attitude is the basis for dynamic teams. Leaders should demonstrate and reward behaviors that promote learning, adaptation, and experimentation. Instead of asking, "Is this person the best fit for the role?" Consider, "How can this person grow into the role?"

2. Concentrate on strengths.

Recognize that each team member brings distinct skills to the table. Use resources such as strength tests or one-on-one meetings to discover and align them with project requirements.

3. Promote cross-functional collaboration.

Break down silos by allowing team members to collaborate across departments and functions. Cross-functional teams organically expose people to new challenges and positions, which promotes development and flexibility.

4. Establish role fluidity in projects.

When starting a project, emphasize that responsibilities are variable and may change depending on the task's developing demands. Create an atmosphere in which people feel secure volunteering for tasks beyond their customary duties.

5. Recognise and reward initiatives.

Celebrate people who venture outside of their comfort zones to contribute in novel ways. Recognition underscores the importance of dynamic contributions and inspires others to follow suit.

Practical Steps for Leaders:

1. Define roles as evolving entities.

Create job descriptions as live documents. Instead of identifying set obligations, identify key areas of responsibility and emphasize flexibility.

2. Create Development Pathways.

Provide training, coaching, and chances for workers to improve skills in a variety of areas. For example, a software engineer who is interested in marketing may attend courses or shadow the marketing department.

3. Encourage collaborative decision-making.

Encourage team members to engage in creating their responsibilities. Regularly enquire, "What do you want to work on next?" in "What untapped skills can you bring to this project?"

4. Use technology to increase flexibility.

Use technologies like talent markets or skill catalogs to increase the visibility of team members' talents. This makes it easy to connect people with possibilities within the organization.

5. Measure and adjust.

Monitor how dynamic contributions affect team performance and individual happiness. Surveys, performance indicators, and feedback sessions may help you adjust your strategy.

Addressing Challenges

The switch to dynamic contributions is not without its challenges. Common problems include reluctance to change, fear of failure, and ambiguity in responsibility.

Strategies for overcoming these challenges:

Begin small: Before scaling up, test the strategy on a single project or team.

Communicate in a transparent manner: Explain the rationale for the change and the advantages it provides to both the organization and the personnel.

Assist: Offer training and guidance to help folks comfortably manage new responsibilities.

Clarify responsibility: Even in dynamic jobs, ensure that accountability for results is explicit to prevent misunderstanding.

Real-world Examples

1. The Google "20% Time" Policy

Google permits workers to devote 20% of their time to initiatives outside of their main tasks. This has resulted in breakthroughs such as Gmail and Google Maps, demonstrating the value of enabling dynamic contributions.

2. IDEO's Flexible Teams.

The design company IDEO is well-known for its project-based methodology, in which staff often switch jobs depending on the demands of each task. This adaptability enhances the firm's reputation for innovation.

3. Startups and Small Businesses.

Many startups adopt dynamic roles out of necessity. Employees often wear many hats, which increases agility and exposes them to a variety of situations that promote development.

## The Future of Work

As technology advances, the need for adaptable, multi-skilled teams will only increase. Leaders who welcome dynamic contributions today are not merely planning for the future but actively influencing it.

By going beyond defined jobs, you enable people to realize their full potential, foster creativity, and create a robust, adaptive organization. In this approach, employment is about more than simply completing a job description; it's about unlocking human potential in service of common objectives.

The issue is not whether to welcome dynamic contributions, but how soon you can start. The future of leadership is about building conditions in which people feel empowered to step up, step in, and succeed.

# From Feedback to Feedforward: Redefining the Conversation for Future Success

Traditional feedback has long been an essential component of personal and professional growth. It assesses previous performance, identifies development opportunities, and establishes a standard for responsibility. However, input often falls short of causing significant change. Why? Because it is fundamentally retroactive, focusing on what has already occurred rather than enabling people to determine what could happen. Enter feedforward, a disruptive strategy that transfers the emphasis from previous performance to future potential. Marshall Goldsmith, a leadership specialist, coined the term "feedforward," which emphasizes concrete, forward-thinking ideas that help people develop and prosper. It is about transitioning from assessment to inspiration, and criticism to empowerment.

Why Feedback Falls Short

Before delving into the fundamentals of feedforward, it's critical to understand why conventional feedback often fails to deliver the desired results.

1. Feedback is rooted in the past

Feedback focuses mostly on previous acts, which may make people feel condemned or defensive. It seldom offers a plan for future achievement.

2. Negative connotations.

Even when presented positively, input might seem like criticism. Employees may concentrate on what went wrong rather than how to improve.

3. Power imbalances.

In hierarchical organizations, feedback often flows downhill, perpetuating a top-down dynamic that inhibits cooperation and innovation.

4. Limited emotional impact.

Feedback talks often concentrate on what was rather than capturing the enthusiasm of what may be. This reduces their potential to motivate change.

5. Ambiguity.

Feedback might be ambiguous or lack specific instructions, leaving people unsure about how to make genuine improvements.

What is Feedforward?

Feedforward is a forward-thinking method for performance enhancement. Instead of analyzing previous behavior, it focuses on future actions and possibilities. It inspires people to consider what they might do differently to obtain better results, resulting in a more positive, solution-focused discourse.

At its foundation, feedforward is about realizing potential, nurturing it, and channeling it for development and success.

Principles of Feedforward

1. Future —Focused feedback focuses on actions that individuals or teams may take going ahead. It changes the narrative from "What went wrong?" to "What's possible?"

2. constructive and positive.

The focus is on strengths and possibilities, which instill confidence and determination to progress.

3. Actionable.

Feedforward makes clear, practical advice that people can put into practice right now.

4. Inclusive

It encourages cooperation and input from all viewpoints to provide well-rounded, effective proposals for improvement.

5) Iterative

Feedforward is not a one-time talk; it is a continuous process that changes as objectives, problems, and opportunities shift.

How Feedforward Drives Growth.

Feedforward has various benefits over conventional feedback, including a more engaging and powerful experience for both people and organizations.

1. Encourages growth. Mindset

Feedforward emphasizes the notion that skills and talents are adaptable. Focussing on the future promotes an attitude of constant learning and progress.

2. Develops Relationships

Feedforward operates collaboratively rather than hierarchically. It fosters an atmosphere of trust and respect, hence developing connections among coworkers, leaders, and teams.

3. Increases Engagement.

Feedforward is positive and solution-oriented, so people feel energized and encouraged rather than criticized.

4. Promotes Innovation

Feedforward promotes creativity and experimentation

by emphasizing possibilities rather than limits.

5. Promotes Clarity.

Feedforward's practical focus helps people realize precisely what measures to take to reach their objectives.

Practical Strategies for Implementing Feedforward

Moving from feedback to feedforward requires a conscious adjustment in mentality and communication habits. Here's how leaders, teams, and organizations can make it happen:

1. Reframe the conversation.

Replace statements like "Let's review what went wrong" with "Let's explore how we can do even better."

Begin talks with questions like:

"What do you think could help you achieve your next goal?"

"What strengths can you leverage to overcome this challenge?"

2. Concentrate on goals.

Orient the debate around future goals. For example:

Rather than reacting with, "You didn't communicate effectively," try this: "How can we ensure clearer communication in the next project?"

3. Be specific and actionable.

Feedforward should offer specific initiatives for improvement. For example:

Rather than stating, "Improve your presentation skills," propose: "In your next presentation, consider using more visuals and practicing transitions to engage your audience."

4. Initiate a collaborative dialogue.

Encourage input from the person getting feedback. Ask open-ended queries like these:

"What ideas do you have for improving in this area?"

"What support do you need to reach your goals?"

5. Integrate into regular practices.

Make feedback a part of your regular check-ins, team meetings, and performance evaluations. This emphasizes its significance and normalizes future-oriented discussions.

Examples of feedforward in action

Scenario 1: Feedback from Team Leader to Employee: "You missed the project deadline."

Feedforward: "For the next project, let's include checkpoints to guarantee we remain on track. What timetable would make you feel more secure in making the deadline?

Scenario 2: Peer-to-Peer Collaboration

Feedback: "Your presentation was not engaging."

Feedforward: "Next time, try beginning with a narrative or a question to capture the audience's attention. What do you think would best suit your style?"

Scenario 3: Manager and Team Feedback: "The team didn't communicate well during the last sprint."

Feedforward: "How can we improve communication in the next sprint?" Would a daily check-in or a shared task board help us keep in sync?"

The Function of Leaders in Feedforward

Leaders play an important role in incorporating feedback into organizational culture. Here's how.

1. Model the behavior.

Leaders should seek feedback themselves, displaying a willingness to develop and change. For instance, ask your team, "What's one thing I could do differently to better support you?"

2. Provide Training Offer training or tools to assist team members in comprehending and successfully applying feedback.

3. Ensure psychological safety.

Create an atmosphere in which people feel comfortable sharing ideas, taking chances, and learning from errors.

4. Recognise and reward.

Celebrate accomplishment and development, highlighting the importance of feedback as a success driver.

From feedforward to transformation.

Feedforward is more than simply a tool for enhancing performance; it is a mindset that changes the way people and organizations think about growth. Focussing on the future fosters creativity, strengthens connections, and uncovers untapped potential.

As the workplace evolves, feedforward provides a strong foundation for managing change and achieving success. It turns the emphasis from what has been to what may be, allowing people to imagine and become their best selves.

The issue is not whether feedforward will replace feedback, but how soon we can adopt this forward-thinking strategy to help our teams reach their full potential. The future awaits, and feedforward is the key to unlocking it.

# From Leading to Learning Together: The Evolution of Effective Teamship

Leadership has typically been perceived as a top-down dynamic in which leaders direct, teach, and make choices while team members carry out responsibilities. However, in today's fast-paced, linked world, this approach is no longer adequate. The most effective teams understand that leadership is more than simply commanding; it is about learning together. This transition from leading to shared learning reflects a significant change in our thinking about cooperation, progress, and success.

The Case for Continuous Learning in Teams.

Work has gotten more complicated, demanding agility, innovation, and adaptation. In this context, no one leader can have all the solutions. Challenges are becoming more unexpected, and solutions often arise via cooperation rather than orders.

1. Shared Ownership of Growth

When leaders and team members commit to learning together, they share responsibility for difficulties and triumphs. This cultivates a culture of mutual respect and responsibility.

2. Adaptive Problem Solving

Teams that learn together are better able to solve complicated issues. They pool their combined expertise, try out ideas, and iterate depending on real-time feedback.

3. Building Resilience

Learning via shared experiences enables teams to overcome uncertainty and recover from failures. It promotes a growth attitude, which views problems as chances for advancement.

4. Fostering Innovation

Collaborative learning promotes creativity. Diverse viewpoints and open debate provide innovations that would never occur in a typical leader-led paradigm.

The Role of Leaders in Learning Together

Leaders are more than simply directors; they are also facilitators, mentors, and learners. Here's how leaders may accept this shift:

1. Be Vulnerable and Open: Leaders who admit they don't have all the answers provide a secure environment for team members to share ideas and thoughts. This humility builds trust and fosters open conversation.

2. Encourage experimentation.

Leaders may create a learning culture by encouraging innovation. Instead of penalizing failures, they present them as chances to learn important lessons.

3. Share the spotlight.

Effective leaders understand that their duty is not to dominate debates, but rather to enhance the opinions of their team. They encourage others to take the initiative by taking a step back.

4. Lead by example.

Leaders who actively seek learning—whether via professional development, criticism, or taking on new challenges—set a strong example for their staff.

The Transition from Leading to Learning Together.

Transforming a team into a learning organization does not happen overnight. It takes conscious action, constant effort, and a willingness to progress.

1. Establish a foundation of trust.

Learning together begins with trust. Team members should feel comfortable discussing ideas, acknowledging errors, and providing constructive criticism. Leaders may build trust by being truthful, consistent, and helpful.

2. Provide opportunities for shared learning.

Workshops & Training: Provide professional dovolopment opportunities for the whole staff.

Cross-functional Collaboration: Encourage team members to learn from one another's skills by collaborating across roles and departments.

Retrospectives: Conduct regular reviews of projects and processes to identify lessons learned and opportunities for improvement.

3. Foster open communication.

Effective learning requires open communication. Teams must feel free to discuss difficulties, share ideas, and debate solutions without fear of repercussions.

4. Embrace Diverse Perspectives

Learning is most effective when it incorporates a diversity of opinions. Diverse teams—across age, gender, culture, and expertise—bring a wealth of ideas, which fuels innovation and development.

5. Celebrate progress.

Recognise and celebrate milestones along the learning path. Recognizing achievement, whether it is a little process improvement or a significant breakthrough, underlines the importance of collaborative learning.

The Power of Shared Challenges

Working together to solve problems provides some of the most meaningful learning opportunities. Whether it's meeting a tight deadline, reacting to market changes, or resolving a complicated issue, shared problems provide possibilities for development.

Shared accountability: When teams tackle issues together, they form a feeling of collective accountability.

Success becomes a shared accomplishment, and failures become shared learning experiences.

Strengthened Bonds: Overcoming difficulty as a team improves connections, generating a feeling of camaraderie and trust that goes beyond the present issue.

Accelerated Growth: Challenges often push people and teams beyond their comfort zones, hastening personal and professional growth.

Real-world Examples of Learning Together

1. Tech startups and agile learning.

Agile approaches in the technology sector demonstrate the value of collaborative learning. Teams regularly iterate on their products, learning from each sprint and integrating input to improve. Leaders in these situations value cooperation and agility, ensuring that the team evolves with the product.

2. Healthcare Teams. During crises.

During the COVID-19 pandemic, healthcare workers throughout the globe highlighted the value of collaborative learning. Physicians, nurses, and administrators collaborated to adjust to changing recommendations, discuss best practices, and develop solutions in real-time.

3. Sports Teams and Dynamic Roles.

Successful sports teams often embrace the concept of collaborative learning. Coaches and players watch game films, analyze strategies, and adjust their tactics based on their combined knowledge. Leaders on the pitch, such as captains, develop with their colleagues, adding to the team's overall success.

The Future of Teamwork: Continuous Learning as a Way of Life

Effective teamwork is more than a set hierarchy or static positions; it is a dynamic, growing collaboration in which leaders and team members learn from and with one another. This continuous learning approach helps teams remain nimble, inventive, and resilient in the face of change.

In this paradigm, leaders are not simply the ones driving the ship; they are also co-navigators, charting a path with their crew. They serve as mentors, sounding boards, and fellow learners, inspiring progress via their example.

When teams embrace learning together, they may reach their greatest potential. Challenges turn stepping stones, wins become community victories, and development into a collaborative journey. This is the core of contemporary leadership: not just leading but walking with others.

As we progress in an ever-changing environment, the

most successful teams will be those who prioritize learning over leadership, collaboration over control, and collective development above individual glory. Because, ultimately, genuine leadership isn't about being the brightest person in the room; it's about creating an environment in which everyone can be their smartest, best self.

# Conclusion: From Solo Leadership to Team Empowerment – Embracing a New Era of Leadership

The landscape of leadership has changed dramatically. What was once a lonely endeavor focused on individual vision and authority has transformed into a dynamic, collaborative process in which the collective strength of the team takes precedence over the uniqueness of the leader. Modern leaders are learning that their greatest strength is engaging, motivating, and empowering their people from the inside, rather than leading them from above.

This change takes more than simply a mental shift; it necessitates a thorough reconsideration of what leadership entails. The age of the infallible, all-knowing leader has gone, giving way to the collaborative leader, who emphasizes shared ownership, various viewpoints, and adaptability. Empowered teams are no longer a luxury in today's complicated, linked world; they are a must.

The ripple effects of empowerment

Empowered teams do more than simply improve results; they change the fundamental fabric of an organization. They promote a culture of creativity, resilience, and responsibility. These teams create self-sustaining ecosystems in which everyone participates, learns, and develops by spreading leadership and empowering people to use their skills.

Modern leaders that embrace empowerment have a rippling effect:

1. Improved Collaboration: Team members actively communicate with one another, harnessing their skills to generate synergy.

2. Increased Innovation: Creativity thrives when people have different points of view and work together to solve problems.

3. Improved Morale: Empowered employees feel respected, engaged, and committed to the team's objective.

4. Greater Adaptability: Teams that share responsibility and ownership are more responsive to change.

These ripple effects benefit not just the organization, but also its consumers, stakeholders, and the larger community. Empowered teams produce solutions that are not just successful, but also long-term and meaningful.

10 Transformative Shifts as Catalysts of Change

Throughout this investigation on transformative leadership changes, eleven principles have emerged as guiding lights for contemporary leaders. These shifts—from command to cooperation, from control to trust, and from controlling performance to fostering growth—provide a road map for 21st-century leadership.

However, these changes are not one-time modifications. They are continuing commitments to reimagining leadership as a collaborative process rather than a single one. They need leaders to:

Give up the appearance of control in favor of building trust and autonomy.

Create an atmosphere of psychological safety in which chances are taken and failures are seen as learning opportunities.

Change their emphasis from short-term outcomes to long-term growth and success.

Leadership is a shared journey.

Finally, leadership in the current day entails getting off the pedestal and entering the circle. It is about accepting the fact that no one individual can have all of the information, skills, or solutions required to face today's difficulties. The most effective leaders allow others to flourish, develop, and lead alongside them.

This move increases rather than diminishes the leader's function. By enabling their colleagues, leaders unleash possibilities much bigger than their contributions. They become the builders of a culture that fosters innovation, makes resiliency second nature, and shares success.

Call to Action for Modern Leaders

As we complete our examination of revolutionary

leadership transformations, the call to action is clear: modern leaders must be willing to rethink, relearn, and reinvent what leadership entails. Empowerment is not a sign of weakness; rather, it represents the ultimate strength. It requires bravery to trust others, wisdom to appreciate many perspectives, and humility to lead through service.

Leadership is no longer about standing separate from the team; it is about standing with them. It is about transitioning from individual accomplishments to group successes, from hierarchical authority to shared purpose, and from static leadership to dynamic progress.

In today's society, successful leadership requires empowering oneself as well as others. It is about realizing each team member's full potential and enjoying the collective strength. This is more than simply a change in leadership; it is a revolution.

And this is a revolution worth leading.

Enter this new age not as a lone leader, but as an enabling force that changes teams, organizations, and individuals. This is the future of leadership, and it starts with you.

# Appendix: Practical Tools and Resources for Team Empowerment

The journey from solo leadership to team empowerment involves more than theoretical knowledge; it necessitates tangible tactics, tools, and practices that leaders can put into effect in real-world circumstances. This appendix serves as a thorough roadmap for leaders to traverse the ten transformational changes, including templates, activities, and tools for driving significant change.

1. From Command to Collaboration: Developing Synergy

Key Practice: Create collaborative frameworks.

RACI Matrix (Responsible, Accountable, Consulted, and Informed)

Use this tool to define roles and duties within a team, ensuring that cooperation is organized and effective.

Activity: Weekly Collaboration Retrospectives.

Hold weekly team meetings to reflect on their joint efforts, evaluate what went well, and suggest areas for growth.

Resource: Books

General Stanley McChrystal is the author of Team of Teams: New Rules of Engagement for a Complex World.

2. From Control to Trust: Establishing Psychological Safety

Transparency is a key practice for increasing trust.

Exercise: Trust Radar.

Ask team members to anonymously rank their confidence in leadership and coworkers. Use the findings to discover your strengths and areas for improvement.

Trust-Building Workshops

Organize team-building activities that emphasize vulnerability and mutual understanding, such as telling personal experiences or working together to solve problems.

Resource: Books

Patrick Lencioni's "The Five Dysfunctions of a Team"

3. From Task Management to Inspiring Purpose

Key Practice: Link team objectives to a broader purpose.

Exercise: Purpose Mapping

Create a visual map that connects individual activities to organizational ideals and larger social implications.

Activity: Purpose Spotlights

Highlight team members who are aligned with the organization's goal and

highlight how their work fits into the wider picture.
Resource: Videos
Simon Sinek's TED Talk: Start with Why.
4. From directing performance to guiding growth
Key Practice: Develop a coaching attitude.
Tool: GROW Model.
Use this framework—Goals, Reality, Options, and Will—to organize coaching interactions and help team members reach their full potential.
Activity: One-on-one coaching sessions
Schedule frequent, devoted time with team members to talk about their professional progress and personal goals.
Resource: Courses
Online coaching courses are available on sites such as LinkedIn Learning and Coursera.
5. Transition from Individual Decisions to Inclusive Consensus
Key Practice: Encourage diverse decision-making.

Tool: Six Thinking Hats by Edward de Bono.
Use this framework to assess choices from a variety of angles, guaranteeing inclusive and well-rounded outcomes.
Activity: Decision Forums
Organize forums in which team members submit ideas and assess the benefits and drawbacks before making final choices.
Resource: Books
Patterson, Grenny, et al. provide Crucial Conversations: Tools for Talking When Stakes Are High.
6. From Fixed Roles to Dynamic Contributions.
Key Practice: Accept role flexibility.
Exercise: Skills Audit.
Periodically evaluate team members' abilities, interests, and goals to uncover possibilities for them to take on additional responsibilities.
Activity: Rotational Responsibilities
Rotate leadership positions in projects or meetings to

expose team members to various tasks.

Resource: Articles.

The Future of Work: Why Job Descriptions are Becoming Obsolete (HBR).

7. From Feedback to Feedforward

Key Practice: Concentrate on future progress.

Exercise: Feedforward Conversations.

Instead of assessing previous achievements, provide precise, concrete recommendations for future success.

Activity: Feedforward sessions.

Schedule team meetings to discuss constructive suggestions for development, with each member giving at least one forward-thinking recommendation.

Resource: Workshops

Marshall Goldsmith provides Leadership Feedforward Training.

8. From Individual Problem Solving to Collective Innovation

Key Practice: Encourage team inventiveness.

Tool: Brainstorming Canvas.

Use a structured brainstorming template to generate and analyze ideas collectively.

Activity: Innovation Challenges.

Set up monthly contests in which teams submit new solutions to current issues, with minor prizes for the most original ideas.

Resource: Books

Tom Kelley and David Kelley wrote the book Creative Confidence: Unleashing the Creative Potential Within Us All.

9. From Transactional Relationships to Transformational Connections.

Key Practice: Develop stronger team connections.

Exercise: Connection Circles.

Create a platform for team members to express their personal and professional highlights, establishing a feeling of community and empathy.

Activity: Mentorship Programs Pair senior team members with juniors to foster cross-level relationships and mentoring possibilities.

Resource: Books Dare to Lead, by Brené Brown.

10. Transitioning from solo leadership to team empowerment.

Key Practice: Redefining leadership as a shared duty.

Exercise: Leadership Roundtables Rotate leadership roles during meetings or projects to disperse authority and foster a feeling of responsibility.

Activity: Empowerment Audits.

Regularly assess if team members feel empowered to take the initiative and make choices. Adjust procedures to increase autonomy.

Resource: Books Turn the Ship Around, by L. David Marquet.

More Resources for Team Empowerment

1. Online platforms for team collaboration.

Slack, Trello, and Asana: Encourage communication and project management in collaborative settings.

2. Training Programs.

Dale Carnegie's leadership courses emphasize teamwork and empowerment.

Harvard Business Review Online Leadership Courses.

3. Professional Organisations.

The Society for Human Resource Management (SHRM) provides resources on leadership development.

The Centre for Creative Leadership (CCL) provides empowerment-focused leadership training.

4. Recommended Reading List

Simon Sinek wrote the book Leaders Eat Last.

The Empowerment Manual: A Guide for Collaborative Groups, by Starhawk.

Daniel Coyle wrote The Culture Code: The Secrets of Highly Successful Groups.

Final Thoughts

Empowerment is more than simply a plan; it is a commitment to maximizing team performance and cultivating a culture of shared success. By accepting these changes, leaders may not only alter their teams but also rethink what leadership means in the current day. Use these tools, resources, and practices to assist you through this transforming journey. Together, the possibilities are unlimited.

www.ingramcontent.com/pod-product-compliance
Lightning Source LLC
Chambersburg PA
CBHW071518220526
45472CB00003B/1068